# OUR
# ROAD READY RECORDS

Important Information About
Our Life, Estate, and Wishes

····································································

NAME AND DATE

····································································

NAME AND DATE

## CONFIDENTIAL

This portfolio contains confidential information
and should be stored in a safe place.

Published by 55 Plus Essential Services, LLC
www.55PlusES.com
Copyright © 2023 Susan Loumagne

Author: Susan Loumagne

ISBN: 979-8-9867618-7-9 (paperback)

# TABLE OF CONTENTS

**This planner is not a legal document and cannot
be considered a Will or any other legal document.**

# HELLO RVERS,

*Road Ready Records is a space-saving booklet to take on the road for quick access to your personal information, and you won't need to depend on a WiFi signal. It's also useful for family members to know your wishes.*

*This record book has spaces for two people. Person specific pages are noted by One or Two.*

*Recommendations:*

- *For information specific to your RV, we recommend you purchase a maintenance log book and keep your owner's manual handy.*

- *Always travel with a current hard-copy atlas. You can't always depend on Internet connections and electronic navigation.*

- *Fill in only the sections that apply to you.*

- *Use the "To Do Notes" to keep a list of what you need to do, find, or replace.*

- *Review the Security and Storage section to keep your confidential information safe while on the road.*

- *If you need a will or other must-have documents, take the time to create those. Consider one of the services on the Resource Pages.*

- *Completing this Guide prompts a reflection on past decisions about coverages or choices, helping you determine their relevance.*

- *Let key people know you have this Guide and where it's stored.*

- *Visit our website to purchase a digital version of the Portfolio and companion items.   www.RoadReadyRecords.com*

*Happy Travels ~*

# QUICK START GUIDE TO COMPLETING YOUR ROAD-READY RECORDS

## 1: Schedule It

Block off time this week to begin your Guide. At the end of the session, schedule the time you will work on the next sections.

## 2: Do It

You may want to work with a partner. One person writes while the other dictates information. Only fill in the information that applies to you and you feel comfortable adding. You may use only the last four digits of your credit card.

## 3: To-Do List

Use the To-Do page to list what information and documents you need to find, copy, or replace.

## 4: Photo and Video It

Take photos of your family and pets for identification purposes. In addition, take pictures and videos of your RV and your home's contents and exterior so you'll have a visual record for yourself and insurance claims.

## 5: Follow Up

Order copies of missing documents and complete all lingering tasks on your list. The Resource Page has links to help you obtain originals of any essential missing cards or documents.

## 6: Store It

We recommend storing this Guide with your essential legal and estate documents, photos, letters to loved ones, and other necessary and important items you've referenced.

## 7: Share It

Let trusted people know that you have this Guide and where it is stored. It is also the perfect time to initiate hard-to-have conversations to discuss your estate and let people know your wishes.

# STORING YOUR IMPORTANT DOCUMENTS AND CONFIDENTIAL INFORMATION

## Introduction

Immediate access to vital information for day-to-day living and emergencies. Road Ready Records ensures you'll have what you need when you need it.

Storing confidential information and important documents in your RV requires planning and organization. The guidelines below offer suggestions to meet different needs based on how often you use your RV—full-time, part-time, or just for weekends.

## Classification: Full-Time, Part-Time, Weekender

Your RV usage frequency will determine which documents need to be at hand.

- Full-Time RVers: Store Road Ready Records along with all your essential documents since your RV is your primary residence.
- Part-Time/Weekender RVers: Travel with Road Ready Records, and only those documents essential for short trips or emergencies.

## What to Store?

Depending on your RV's role as a residence or leisure vehicle, you'll need to determine the documents you need to keep with you. Legal considerations may also influence whether to keep originals or copies.

- Insurance Papers and Information
- Will, Power of Attorney, and Healthcare Directive
- RV Photos and Videos: For identification and insurance claims
- Personal Photos and Videos: For sentimental value or identification

# STORING YOUR IMPORTANT DOCUMENTS AND CONFIDENTIAL INFORMATION

## Information Storage

Safety, accessibility, and ease of use will influence the choice of storage medium.

- Hard Copies: Use a binder or folder for original or copied documents.
- Digital Storage Options:
  - Computer Hard Drives: Secure with passwords or encryption.
  - Tablets: Secure with passwords.
  - USB Thumb Drives: Handy for storing photos and videos.
    (Available on our website.RoadReadyRecords.com)
- Cloud Storage: May be inaccessible without consistent internet connectivity.

## Where to Store for Easy Access

The storage location within your RV should be easily accessible while also offering protection from environmental factors. Consider storing documents in the interior of your RV to protect against heat and humidity.

- Locked Compartment: Extra security and easy access.
- RV Lockbox: Offers excellent security and could be permanently fixed.
- Waterproof Container: Protection against moisture.

## Secondary Storage Location

For full-time RVers, having a secondary storage location is prudent, especially considering the increasing incidence of natural disasters.

- Safety Deposit Box: At a bank or other secure facility.
- Friend/Family Member's Home: Using a waterproof/fireproof lockbox for extra protection.
- Document Duplication: Keep a second set of all essential documents for redundancy.

# STORING YOUR IMPORTANT DOCUMENTS
# AND CONFIDENTIAL INFORMATION

## Storage Ideas

- Decentralized Cloud Storage: Dropbox, Google Drive, One Drive. Ensure you use the encryption feature for data security and privacy.

- Biometric Security: Using biometrically locked safes for storing essential documents.

- Digital Notary Services: Using online platforms to notarize essential documents, thereby maintaining their legal status when stored digitally.

- LYubico YubiKey 5 Series: For two-factor authentication on digital devices.

- Filecoin: For decentralized cloud storage.

## Product Recommendations

Visit RoadReadyRecords.com

# RESOURCES

## Vital Records

*Birth, Death, Marriage, and Divorce Records*          www.cdc.gov/nchs/w2w.htm

Link to your state's Bureau of Vital Statistics

## Government Programs

Medicare                                             www.medicare.gov
800-633-4227

Social Security Office                               www.socialsecurity.gov
800-772-1213

Veterans Administration                              www.va.gov
800-827-1000

Veterans Service Records National Archives           www.archives.gov/veterans
866-272-6272

Passports – U.S. Passports                           www.travel.state.gov
877-487-2778

## Estate and Must Have Documents

*Wills, Trusts, Healthcare Directives, and Durable Power of Attorney*

Legal Zoom                                           www.legalzoom.com
800-773-0888

Trust and Will                                       www.trustandwill.com
866-908-7878

## Emergency Preparation & Disaster Relief

American Red Cross                                   www.redcross.org
800-733-2767

FEMA – Federal Emergency Management Association  www.fema.gov
800-621-3362

Ready.gov                                            www.ready.gov
800-621-3362

# RV RESOURCES - APPS AND SITES

## Camping and Staying Spots

Allstays Camp & RV A Comprehensive resource that provides lots of information. Overnights at RV parks, rest areas, plus free sites and other services. Get reviews, a handy map search, and real-time updates on your route!    * Membership

Campendium - This free platform details about 30,000 campsites, including RV parks, state parks, and free camping spots across the U.S.

RV Parky - Crafted by an RV enthusiast, it lists RV parks, campgrounds, and places to rest up for the night.

FreeRoam - Treasure for boondockers. Discover free or budget-friendly camping spots. Plus, safety, weather, cell signal, and more!

Overlander  Your global directory! From camping, hotels, restaurants, and points of interest.

Harvest Hosts/Boondockers - RV travelers can park overnight at cool spots like wineries or museums. A fresh twist from the usual campgrounds.  * Membership

Park4Night - Global favorite!  Find user-shared overnight parking, secret camping spots, and more.

## Travel Directions

Roadtrippers App -  plan your trip and include You're always a short detour from an Extraordinary Place!

RV Life – Similar to Google Maps and made for RVers. Your RV-specialized GPS. Navigate according to your RV's size and get real-time traffic updates.

## RV Newsletter

RV Travel - RVTravel.com - "For 20 years, RVTravel.com has been the #1 news and information source by RVers, for RVers."

# RV RESOURCES - APPS AND SITES

## Helpful Extras

WiFi Map - Stay connected! Locate and access WiFi hot spots globally.

GasBuddy - Save on fuel. Spot the cheapest gas stations nearby.

Flush Toilet Finder - shows the closest bathrooms but not the cleanest.
Read the reviews

Sanidumps -  Especially valuable for RV travelers, Sanidumps helps you locate RV dump stations near you. You can search by city, state, or province.

AccuWeather - Never underestimate the weather! Be prepared for all your adventures, from solar charge opportunities to rain checks.

Speed Test App - For the remote workers. Ensure your campsite has strong internet before setting up.

Facebook - A world of RV communities awaits. From boondocking to women RVers, connect with like-minded individuals and tap into shared knowledge.

## Support Organizations and Clubs

RV Advisor Consumer Association                      www.RVACA.org
833-229-0911

Good Sam - *everything RV*                           www.GoodSam.com

Escapees RV Club                                     www.escapees.com

## Trip Makers - *Where to go and how to get there*

AAA                                                  www.AAA.com
866-636-2377

Rand McNally                              https://tripmaker.randmcnally.com
866-908-7878

## Veterinary
Vet Locator                                          vetlocator.com

# TO DO NOTES

# TO DO NOTES

....................................................................................................

....................................................................................................

....................................................................................................

....................................................................................................

....................................................................................................

....................................................................................................

....................................................................................................

....................................................................................................

....................................................................................................

....................................................................................................

....................................................................................................

....................................................................................................

....................................................................................................

....................................................................................................

....................................................................................................

....................................................................................................

....................................................................................................

....................................................................................................

....................................................................................................

....................................................................................................

....................................................................................................

# TO DO NOTES

# PERSONAL PROFILE - ONE

Name: ..............................................................................................

Birth Date: ...................................... Place of Birth: .............................

Name on Birth Certificate: ...................................................................

Mother's Maiden Name: ........................................ Living? ....................

..............................................................................................

Father's Name: ...................................... Living? ...............................

..............................................................................................

Relationship Status: ............................ Spouse/Partner's Name: ....................

..............................................................................................

Employed By: ...................................................................................

Job Title: ......................................................................................

Supervisor's Name and Phone Number: .......................................................

..............................................................................................

Volunteer Organizations and Contact:.........................................................

..............................................................................................

..............................................................................................

Military Branch: ...................................... Rank: ............:...................

Dates Served and Where? ....................................................................

..............................................................................................

**NOTES** ......................................................................................

..............................................................................................

..............................................................................................

..............................................................................................

# IMPORTANT PAPERS - ONE

Examples of important papers are social security card, birth certificate, passport, driver's license, military DD214, marriage license, divorce record, resident alien card, adoption record, frequent traveler #.

| Type | Number | Stored Where? | Copy Y/N |
|------|--------|---------------|----------|
|      |        |               |          |
|      |        |               |          |
|      |        |               |          |
|      |        |               |          |
|      |        |               |          |
|      |        |               |          |
|      |        |               |          |
|      |        |               |          |
|      |        |               |          |
|      |        |               |          |
|      |        |               |          |

# PERSONAL PROFILE - TWO

Name: ..................................................................................................

Birth Date: ......................................... Place of Birth: ...........................

Name on Birth Certificate: ..............................................................

Mother's Maiden Name: ....................................... Living? ...................
..........................................................................................................

Father's Name: ........................................... Living? ...........................
..........................................................................................................

Relationship Status: ............................... Spouse/Partner's Name: ...................
..........................................................................................................

Employed By: ...................................................................................

Job Title: ..........................................................................................

Supervisor's Name and Phone Number: ...........................................
..........................................................................................................

Volunteer Organizations and Contact:..............................................
..........................................................................................................
..........................................................................................................

Military Branch: ..................................... Rank: .................................

Dates Served and Where? ..................................................................
..........................................................................................................

---

**NOTES** ..........................................................................................
..........................................................................................................
..........................................................................................................
..........................................................................................................

# IMPORTANT PAPERS - TWO

Examples of important papers are social security card, birth certificate, passport, driver's license, military DD214, marriage license, divorce record, resident alien card, adoption record, frequent traveler #.

| Type | Number | Stored Where? | Copy Y/N |
|------|--------|---------------|----------|
|      |        |               |          |
|      |        |               |          |
|      |        |               |          |
|      |        |               |          |
|      |        |               |          |
|      |        |               |          |
|      |        |               |          |
|      |        |               |          |
|      |        |               |          |
|      |        |               |          |
|      |        |               |          |

## SIBLINGS

Name: ............................................................ Birth Date: ........................

Phone: .................................... Living?: ......................................

Email or Address:.......... ................................................................

Name: ............................................................ Birth Date: ........................

Phone: .................................... Living?: ......................................

Email or Address: ................................................................

Name: ............................................................ Birth Date: ........................

Phone: .................................... Living?: ......................................

Email or Address: ................................................................

Name: ............................................................ Birth Date: ........................

Phone: .................................... Living?: ......................................

Email or Address: ................................................................

Name: ............................................................ Birth Date: ........................

Phone: .................................... Living?: ......................................

Email or Address: ................................................................

Name: ............................................................ Birth Date: ........................

Phone: .................................... Living?: ......................................

Email or Address: ................................................................

# CHILDREN

Name of Parents: .................................................................................................

*Social Security Number Optional*

Given Name: .......................................................................................................

Date of Birth: ........................................... Place of Birth: ...........................

SS#: .......................................................... Phone Number: ..........................

Email: ...............................................................................................................

---

Given Name: .......................................................................................................

Date of Birth: ........................................... Place of Birth: ...........................

SS#: .......................................................... Phone Number: ..........................

Email: ...............................................................................................................

---

Given Name: .......................................................................................................

Date of Birth: ........................................... Place of Birth: ...........................

SS#: .......................................................... Phone Number: ..........................

Email: ...............................................................................................................

---

Given Name: .......................................................................................................

Date of Birth: ........................................... Place of Birth: ...........................

SS#: .......................................................... Phone Number: ..........................

Email: ...............................................................................................................

---

Given Name: .......................................................................................................

Date of Birth: ........................................... Place of Birth: ...........................

SS#: .......................................................... Phone Number: ..........................

Email: ...............................................................................................................

# IMPORTANT CONTACTS

Name: ........................................ Relationship: ...............................

Phone: ...................................... Phone: .........................................

Email or Address: ..........................................................................

Name: ........................................ Relationship: ...............................

Phone: ...................................... Phone: .........................................

Email or Address: ..........................................................................

Name: ........................................ Relationship: ...............................

Phone: ......................................Phone: .........................................

Email or Address: ..........................................................................

Name: ........................................ Relationship: ...............................

Phone: ...................................... Phone: .........................................

Email or Address: ..........................................................................

Name: ........................................ Relationship: ...............................

Phone: ...................................... Phone: .........................................

Email or Address: ..........................................................................

Name: ........................................ Relationship: ...............................

Phone: ...................................... Phone: .........................................

Email or Address: ..........................................................................

## IMPORTANT CONTACTS

Name: .................................................. Relationship: ...........................

Phone: ................................................ Phone: ...................................

Email or Address: ..........................................................................

Name: .................................................. Relationship: ...........................

Phone: ................................................ Phone: ...................................

Email or Address: ..........................................................................

Name: .................................................. Relationship: ...........................

Phone: ................................................ Phone: ...................................

Email or Address: ..........................................................................

Name: .................................................. Relationship: ...........................

Phone: ................................................ Phone: ...................................

Email or Address: ..........................................................................

Name: .................................................. Relationship: ...........................

Phone: ................................................ Phone: ...................................

Email or Address: ..........................................................................

Name: .................................................. Relationship: ...........................

Phone: ................................................ Phone: ...................................

Email or Address: ..........................................................................

# FINANCES

**BANKING** *Add log-in information to Password Section*

Name of Bank: .................................................................................................

Branch Location: .............................................................................................

Contact's Name: ......................................................... Phone No: .......................

| Account Type | Account Number * optional | Name on Account |
|---|---|---|
|  |  |  |
|  |  |  |
|  |  |  |

Notes: ..............................................................................................................

Name of Bank: .................................................................................................

Branch Location: .............................................................................................

Contact's Name: ......................................................... Phone No: .......................

| Account Type | Account Number * optional | Name on Account |
|---|---|---|
|  |  |  |
|  |  |  |
|  |  |  |

Notes: ..............................................................................................................

Name of Bank: .................................................................................................

Branch Location: .............................................................................................

Contact's Name: ......................................................... Phone No: .......................

| Account Type | Account Number * optional | Name on Account |
|---|---|---|
|  |  |  |
|  |  |  |
|  |  |  |

Notes: ..............................................................................................................

# CREDIT CARDS

*\* Account number and security code optional.*        *Add log-in information to the Passwords Section.*

Name of Company: ......................................... Phone No: ....................................

Name on Account: ................................................................................................

Account Number: ......................................... Security Code: ...........................

Expiration: ...................................................... Balance Insured: .......................

---

Name of Company: ......................................... Phone No: ....................................

Name on Account: ................................................................................................

Account Number: ......................................... Security Code: ...........................

Expiration: ...................................................... Balance Insured: .......................

---

Name of Company: ......................................... Phone No: ....................................

Name on Account: ................................................................................................

Account Number: ......................................... Security Code: ...........................

Expiration: ...................................................... Balance Insured: .......................

---

Name of Company: ......................................... Phone No: ....................................

Name on Account: ................................................................................................

Account Number: ......................................... Security Code: ...........................

Expiration: ...................................................... Balance Insured: .......................

---

Name of Company: ......................................... Phone No: ....................................

Name on Account: ................................................................................................

Account Number: ......................................... Security Code: ...........................

Expiration: ...................................................... Balance Insured: .......................

# FINANCIAL SERVICES and CD'S

Financial Services Company: ..............................................................

Advisor's Name: ........................................ Phone Number: ..........................

Address: ..................................................................................

Notes: .....................................................................................

..............................................................................................

Advisor's Name: ........................................ Phone Number: ..........................

Address: ..................................................................................

Notes: .....................................................................................

..............................................................................................

# CERTIFICATE OF DEPOSIT

Bank: .......................................................................................

Amount: ......................... Interest Rate: ................ Maturity Date: .....................

Bank: .......................................................................................

Amount: ......................... Interest Rate: ................ Maturity Date: .....................

Bank: .......................................................................................

Amount: ......................... Interest Rate: ................ Maturity Date: .....................

Bank: .......................................................................................

Amount: ......................... Interest Rate: ................ Maturity Date: .....................

# SAVINGS BONDS STORAGE

..............................................................................................

..............................................................................................

..............................................................................................

..............................................................................................

# INVESTMENTS

Investment Type: ................................. * 401K, IRA, Mutual Funds, Stocks, Bitcoin, NFT's

Held By: ....................................................... Phone Number: ...........................

Account Number: ...................................................................................................

Notes:....................................................................................................................

...............................................................................................................................

Investment Type: ................................. * 401K, IRA, Mutual Funds, Stocks, Bitcoin, NFT's

Held By: ....................................................... Phone Number: ...........................

Account Number: ...................................................................................................

Notes:....................................................................................................................

...............................................................................................................................

Investment Type: ................................. * 401K, IRA, Mutual Funds, Stocks, Bitcoin, NFT's

Held By: ....................................................... Phone Number: ...........................

Account Number: ...................................................................................................

Notes:....................................................................................................................

...............................................................................................................................

Investment Type: ................................. * 401K, IRA, Mutual Funds, Stocks, Bitcoin, NFT's

Held By: ....................................................... Phone Number: ...........................

Account Number: ...................................................................................................

Notes:....................................................................................................................

...............................................................................................................................

Investment Type: ................................. * 401K, IRA, Mutual Funds, Stocks, Bitcoin, NFT's

Held By: ....................................................... Phone Number: ...........................

Account Number: ...................................................................................................

Notes:....................................................................................................................

...............................................................................................................................

# PERSONAL INCOME

*This section covers any income you receive; salary, social security, pensions, annuities, military, trusts, royalties, bonuses, dividends, interest, alimony, or any other income you receive.*

Type:* ..............................................................................................................

Company: ........................................................ Phone: ..............................

Amount: .................................................. Note: ..........................................

Type:* ..............................................................................................................

Company: ........................................................ Phone: ..............................

Amount: .................................................. Note: ..........................................

Type:* ..............................................................................................................

Company: ........................................................ Phone: ..............................

Amount: .................................................. Note: ..........................................

Type:* ..............................................................................................................

Company: ........................................................ Phone: ..............................

Amount: .................................................. Note: ..........................................

Type:* ..............................................................................................................

Company: ........................................................ Phone: ..............................

Amount: .................................................. Note: ..........................................

Type:* ..............................................................................................................

Company: ........................................................ Phone: ..............................

Amount: .................................................. Note: ..........................................

Type:* ..............................................................................................................

Company: ........................................................ Phone: ..............................

Amount: .................................................. Note: ..........................................

## LOANS YOU OWE

Loan From: ......................................... Phone: ..................................

Account Number: ..............................................................................

Type of Loan: ..................................... Interest Rate: ......................

Amount: .............................................. Payment: ...............................

Date of Origination: ............................... Length of Loan: ..................

Loan From: ......................................... Phone: ..................................

Account Number: ..............................................................................

Type of Loan: ..................................... Interest Rate: ......................

Amount: .............................................. Payment: ...............................

Date of Origination: ............................... Length of Loan: ..................

Loan From: ......................................... Phone: ..................................

Account Number: ..............................................................................

Type of Loan: ..................................... Interest Rate: ......................

Amount: .............................................. Payment: ...............................

Date of Origination: ............................... Length of Loan: ..................

## LOAN AGREEMENTS - Money you are owed

The following are loans that you have given to other people or companies.

To Whom: ....................................... Amount: ...............................

Contact Information: ........................................................................

What are the details of the loan and where is the Promissory Note?

......................................................................................................

To Whom: ....................................... Amount: ...............................

Contact Information: ........................................................................

What are the details of the loan and where is the Promissory Note?

......................................................................................................

# INSURANCE

## RV INSURANCE - make and model, VIN# is added to the Assets section.

Company: ................................................ Phone: ..............................................

Policy Number: ........................ Policy Stored Where? .............................................

Agent Name: ................................................ Agent Phone: ..............................

Notes:................................................................................................................

## AUTO INSURANCE

Company: ................................................ Phone: ..............................................

Policy Number: ........................ Policy Stored Where? .............................................

Agent Name: ................................................ Agent Phone: ..............................

Notes:................................................................................................................

## HEALTH, DENTAL, AND PRESCRIPTION INSURANCE

Name on Policy: ...................................................................................................

Company: ................................................ Phone: ..............................................

Policy Number:........................................ Coverage Details: ...................................

................................................................................................................

Notes:................................................................................................................

Name on Policy: ...................................................................................................

Company: ................................................ Phone: ..............................................

Policy Number:........................................ Coverage Details: ...................................

................................................................................................................

Notes:................................................................................................................

Name on Policy: ...................................................................................................

Company: ................................................ Phone: ..............................................

Policy Number:........................................ Coverage Details: ...................................

................................................................................................................

Notes:................................................................................................................

# LIFE INSURANCE

Name on Policy: .................................................................................................

Company: ........................................... Phone Number: ...............................

Agent: ................................................. Phone Number: ...............................

Policy Number: .............................. Policy Stored Where? ..............................

Amount: ............................... Whole Life or Term: ........... Length of Policy: ...........

Notes: ............................................................................................................

Beneficiary Name: ...................................... Phone Number: ........................

Beneficiary Address: .............................. Aware of Designation? ........................

Contingent Name: ................................................ Phone Number: ...........................

Name on Policy: .................................................................................................

Company: ........................................... Phone Number: ...............................

Agent: ................................................. Phone Number: ...............................

Policy Number: .............................. Policy Stored Where? ..............................

Amount: ............................... Whole Life or Term: ........... Length of Policy: ...........

Notes: ............................................................................................................

Beneficiary Name: ...................................... Phone Number: ........................

Beneficiary Address: .............................. Aware of Designation? ........................

Contingent Name: ................................................ Phone Number: ...........................

Do you have other employee/retiree supplemental life insurance plans? Yes/No
Plan Name: ......................................................................................................

Details: .........................................................................................................

Do you have other employee/retiree supplemental life insurance plans? Yes/No
Plan Name: ......................................................................................................

Details: .........................................................................................................

## ADDITIONAL INSURANCE

Type: ...............................................................................................

Company: ........................................... Amount: .....................................

Policy Number: ........................................ Stored? ................................

Agent Name: ......................................... Phone Number: ......................

Notes: ...............................................................................................

Type: ...............................................................................................

Company: ........................................... Amount: .....................................

Policy Number: ........................................ Stored? ................................

Agent Name: ......................................... Phone Number: ......................

Notes: ...............................................................................................

Type: ...............................................................................................

Company: ........................................... Amount: .....................................

Policy Number: ........................................ Stored? ................................

Agent Name: ......................................... Phone Number: ......................

Notes: ...............................................................................................

Type: ...............................................................................................

Company: ........................................... Amount: .....................................

Policy Number: ........................................ Stored? ................................

Agent Name: ......................................... Phone Number: ......................

Notes: ...............................................................................................

Type: ...............................................................................................

Company: ........................................... Amount: .....................................

Policy Number: ........................................ Stored? ................................

Agent Name: ......................................... Phone Number: ......................

Notes: ...............................................................................................

## INCOME TAX FILING

Accountant's Name: ......................................................................................

Accountant's Phone Number: .........................................................................

Accountant's Address: ...................................................................................

Online Tax Service ........................................................................................

...................................................................................................................

...................................................................................................................

...................................................................................................................

Where do you store copies of previous years? ..............................................

## ADDITIONAL FINANCIAL INFORMATION

Notes:..........................................................................................................

...................................................................................................................

...................................................................................................................

...................................................................................................................

...................................................................................................................

...................................................................................................................

...................................................................................................................

...................................................................................................................

...................................................................................................................

...................................................................................................................

...................................................................................................................

...................................................................................................................

...................................................................................................................

...................................................................................................................

...................................................................................................................

...................................................................................................................

...................................................................................................................

...................................................................................................................

...................................................................................................................

...................................................................................................................

...................................................................................................................

# ASSETS

## REAL ESTATE

Property Type: ................................................ Home, Investment, Rental, Vacation

Address: ............................................................................................................

Purchase Date: ............................................. Payment: .......................

Mortgage Held By: ...........................................................................................

Balance of Loan: ........................................... As of date: .......................

Value of Property: ......................................... As of date: .......................

Homeowners Insurance Company: ....................................................................

Property Tax Amount-How are they paid?: ........................................................

_____

Property Type: ................................................ Home, Investment, Rental, Vacation

Address: ............................................................................................................

Purchase Date: ............................................. Payment: .......................

Mortgage Held By: ...........................................................................................

Balance of Loan: ........................................... As of date: .......................

Value of Property: ......................................... As of date: .......................

Homeowners Insurance Company: ....................................................................

Property Tax Amount-How are they paid?: ........................................................

_____

Property Type: ................................................ Home, Investment, Rental, Vacation

Address: ............................................................................................................

Purchase Date: ............................................. Payment: .......................

Mortgage Held By: ...........................................................................................

Balance of Loan: ........................................... As of date: .......................

Value of Property: ......................................... As of date: .......................

Homeowners Insurance Company: ....................................................................

Property Tax Amount-How are they paid?: ........................................................

## STORAGE OF CODES, KEYS AND PROPERTY

Door Code:...............................................Secuirty System Code:.................................

Where do you keep extra keys for your RV, house, cars? .......................................

...................................................................................................................

...................................................................................................................

Do you have a Storage Unit?  Details: .................................................................

...................................................................................................................

## DOCUMENT AND VALUABLES STORAGE

Do you have a Safe Deposit Box?  Y/N      Where is it?      Where is code or key?

...................................................................................................................

Do you have a Fireproof Lockbox? Y/N        Where is it?      Where is code or key?

...................................................................................................................

## STORED ASSETS

*Don't let your hidden assets be lost forever. Include information about any secret locations here. Or, write down the details and store them in a safety deposit or lockbox to protect your assets.*

Do you have assets hidden in your home?   Y/N  Where? .....................................

Does anyone else know the location?   Y/N   If yes, who? .......................................

If no one else knows, you should share the location or an obvious hint.

Location or hint? ............................................................................................

...................................................................................................................

Do you have assets stored in another location?   Y/N Where? .............................

Does anyone else know the location?  Y/N  If yes, who? .......................................

If no one else knows, you should share the location or give an obvious hint.

Location or hint? ............................................................................................

...................................................................................................................

# VEHICLES

Vehicle Type: ........................................ * Automobile, RV, Boat, Motorcycle, Truck

Make: ................................. Model: ............................. Year: ...........................

Registered To: ................................................... VIN#: ...........................

Status of Ownership: ................................................. Title Stored? .....................

---

Vehicle Type: ........................................ * Automobile, RV, Boat, Motorcycle, Truck

Make: ................................. Model: ............................. Year: ...........................

Registered To: ................................................... VIN#: ...........................

Status of Ownership: ................................................. Title Stored? .....................

---

Vehicle Type: ........................................ * Automobile, RV, Boat, Motorcycle, Truck

Make: ................................. Model: ............................. Year: ...........................

Registered To: ................................................... VIN#: ...........................

Status of Ownership: ................................................. Title Stored? .....................

---

Vehicle Type: ........................................ * Automobile, RV, Boat, Motorcycle, Truck

Make: ................................. Model: ............................. Year: ...........................

Registered To: ................................................... VIN#: ...........................

Status of Ownership: ................................................. Title Stored? .....................

---

Vehicle Type: ........................................ * Automobile, RV, Boat, Motorcycle, Truck

Make: ................................. Model: ............................. Year: ...........................

Registered To: ................................................... VIN#: ...........................

Status of Ownership: ................................................. Title Stored? .....................

# ADDITIONAL INFORMATION ABOUT ASSETS

........................................................................................................

........................................................................................................

........................................................................................................

........................................................................................................

........................................................................................................

........................................................................................................

........................................................................................................

........................................................................................................

........................................................................................................

........................................................................................................

........................................................................................................

........................................................................................................

........................................................................................................

........................................................................................................

........................................................................................................

........................................................................................................

........................................................................................................

........................................................................................................

........................................................................................................

........................................................................................................

........................................................................................................

........................................................................................................

........................................................................................................

........................................................................................................

........................................................................................................

# PERSONAL PROPERTY

*This section covers different categories of items, such as jewelry, coins, firearms, artwork, collectibles, etc. We recommend you have your items appraised and obtain the proper insurance to cover them in case of loss due to theft, flood, fire, or natural disaster.*

Category Name: ......................................................................................

Have you had any of the items appraised?   Y/N

Do you have an insurance rider on any of these items?   Y/N

Have you videotaped or photographed any of these items?   Y/N

Where are the photos and/or videos stored? .............................................

Notes or list items: ..............................................................................

......................................................................................

......................................................................................

......................................................................................

......................................................................................

Category Name: ......................................................................................

Have you had any of the items appraised?   Y/N

Do you have an insurance rider on any of these items?   Y/N

Have you videotaped or photographed any of these items?   Y/N

Where are the photos and/or videos stored? .............................................

Notes or list items: ..............................................................................

......................................................................................

......................................................................................

......................................................................................

......................................................................................

## PERSONAL PROPERTY

Category Name: ..................................................................................

Have you had any of the items appraised?   Y/N

Do you have an insurance rider on any of these items?   Y/N

Have you videotaped or photographed any of these items?   Y/N

Where are the photos and/or videos stored? ...................................

Notes or list items: ..........................................................................

..................................................................................................

..................................................................................................

..................................................................................................

..................................................................................................

..................................................................................................

Use additional pages to list more items.

..................................................................................................

..................................................................................................

..................................................................................................

..................................................................................................

..................................................................................................

..................................................................................................

..................................................................................................

..................................................................................................

..................................................................................................

..................................................................................................

..................................................................................................

..................................................................................................

..................................................................................................

# ESTATE & LEGAL DOCUMENTS
# WILL, TRUST, AND POA - ONE

My attorney is: .............................................. Phone: ...........................................

## WILL

*An attorney is an excellent person to advise you on your Will and ensure that you protect your estate from being overtaxed. In addition, your Will should be kept up-to-date to reflect changes in your family and assets.*

Attorney who handled the Will: ...................................... Phone: .........................
At the law firm of: ...........................................................................................
Last Will is dated: ...........................................................................................
The executor/executrix is: ...............................................................................
Are they aware they are the executor? ............................................................
Have you discussed the Will with them? ...........................................................
*Remind your executor to request multiple copies of your death certificate for accessing your accounts.*

My Will is stored: ........................................ A copy is stored: ...........................
Notes:.............................................................................................................
.......................................................................................................................

## ESTABLISHING A TRUST

*It may be appropriate to seek your attorney's and financial advisor's advice to determine if establishing a trust fund would benefit your situation.*

Do you have a trust? .......................................................................................
Title of the trust: ............................................................................................
Trustees and contact information: ....................................................................

## DURABLE FINANCIAL POWER OF ATTORNEY

*A power of attorney gives someone else (your "Agent") the authority to act on your behalf, while you are living, if you become unable to make decisions for yourself, even for a short period. On your financial POA, you can specify the areas where you want to give power to someone else. Upon your death, the executor takes over.*

Do you have a financial POA? ............................................ Effective when? ............
Name of your Agent? ........................................................................................
Where is your financial POA stored? .................................................................

# LIVING WILL AND HEALTH CARE POWER OF ATTORNEY - ONE

*A living will and health care power of attorney instruct family members and physicians on what steps you want to take should you become unable to make health care decisions. Copies are typically only accepted if your living will specifies they are. You should distribute copies or originals to your family, physician, and attorney.*

## LIVING WILL OR MEDICAL DIRECTIVE

Do you have a Living Will Declaration?................. Effective when?... .....................

Do you a DNR? ...........................................................................................

To carry out my Living Will, I designate: ...........................................................

Have you discussed your wishes with them? ......................................................

The alternate agent is: .................................................................................

My Living Will has been given to: ....................................................................

A copy is stored: .........................................................................................

## HEALTH CARE POWER OF ATTORNEY

Do you have a Health Care Power of Attorney? ....................................................

Effective when? ..........................................................................................

I designate as my Health Care POA: ................................................................

Have you discussed your wishes with them? ......................................................

The alternate agent is: .................................................................................

My Health Care Directive has been given to: ......................................................

A copy is stored: .........................................................................................

## ORGAN DONATION

I do............................ I do not............................ want any of my organs donated.

I want only the following organs donated: ..........................................................
.................................................................................................................

Notes:........................................................................................................
.................................................................................................................

# ESTATE & LEGAL DOCUMENTS
# WILL, TRUST, AND POA - TWO

My attorney is: ............................................. Phone: .......................................

## WILL

*An attorney is an excellent person to advise you on your Will and ensure that you protect your estate from being overtaxed. In addition, your Will should be kept up-to-date to reflect changes in your family and assets.*

Attorney who handled the Will: ...................................... Phone: ........................
At the law firm of: ......................................................................................
Last Will is dated: ......................................................................................
The executor/executrix is: ...........................................................................
Are they aware they are the executor? ............................................................
Have you discussed the Will with them? .........................................................
*Remind your executor to request multiple copies of your death certificate for accessing your accounts.*

My Will is stored: ..................................... A copy is stored: ...........................
Notes:......................................................................................................
..............................................................................................................

## ESTABLISHING A TRUST

*It may be appropriate to seek your attorney's and financial advisor's advice to determine if establishing a trust fund would benefit your situation.*

Do you have a trust? ..................................................................................
Title of the trust: ......................................................................................
Trustees and contact information: .................................................................

## DURABLE FINANCIAL POWER OF ATTORNEY

*A power of attorney gives someone else (your "Agent") the authority to act on your behalf, while you are living, if you become unable to make decisions for yourself, even for a short period. On your financial POA, you can specify the areas where you want to give power to someone else. Upon your death, the executor takes over.*

Do you have a financial POA? ........................................... Effective when? .............
Name of your Agent? .................................................................................
Where is your financial POA stored? ..............................................................

# LIVING WILL AND HEALTH CARE POWER OF ATTORNEY - TWO

*A living will and health care power of attorney instruct family members and physicians on what steps you want to take should you become unable to make health care decisions. Copies are typically only accepted if your living will specifies they are. You should distribute copies or originals to your family, physician, and attorney.*

## LIVING WILL OR MEDICAL DIRECTIVE

Do you have a Living Will Declaration?................ Effective when?... .....................

Do you a DNR? ...........................................................................................................

To carry out my Living Will, I designate: ..................................................................

Have you discussed your wishes with them? ...........................................................

The alternate agent is: ..............................................................................................

My Living Will has been given to: .............................................................................

A copy is stored: ........................................................................................................

## HEALTH CARE POWER OF ATTORNEY

Do you have a Health Care Power of Attorney? .......................................................

Effective when? .........................................................................................................

I designate as my Health Care POA: ........................................................................

Have you discussed your wishes with them? ...........................................................

The alternate agent is: .............................................................................................

My Health Care Directive has been given to: ..........................................................

A copy is stored: .......................................................................................................

## ORGAN DONATION

I do............................ I do not............................ want any of my organs donated.

I want only the following organs donated: ...............................................................
....................................................................................................................................

Notes:.........................................................................................................................
....................................................................................................................................

# MEDICAL INFORMATION - ONE

Name: ............................................................ Date ........................

Blood Type ................................. Height ........................ Weight ........................

**DOCTORS** *(General Practitioner, Dentist, Specialists, Audiology, Internist, Cardiology)*

Doctor: ............................................. Specialty: .................................

Phone: ........................................................................................

Doctor: ............................................. Specialty: .................................

Phone: ........................................................................................

Doctor: ............................................. Specialty: .................................

Phone: ........................................................................................

Doctor: ............................................. Specialty: .................................

Phone: ........................................................................................

\* PATIENT PORTAL INFORMATION – add to PASSWORDS

Veterans Administration Facility: ................................. Phone: ........................

............................................................................................

Dentist: ................................................. Phone: ..............................

Eye Doctor: ............................................. Phone: ..............................

## MEDICAL EQUIPMENT

Do you use medical equipment? ............................... ........................

Who is the supplier? ........................................................................

Details? ....................................................................................

............................................................................................

## MEDICAL CONDITIONS  - ONE

Do you have any medical conditions or hereditary risk factors that require monitoring?

Please give details. ..................................................................................................

...........................................................................................................................

...........................................................................................................................

...........................................................................................................................

...........................................................................................................................

Do you have any allergies? Please give details.

...........................................................................................................................

...........................................................................................................................

## VACCINES AND IMMUNIZATIONS - Type and Date Received

...........................................................................................................................

...........................................................................................................................

...........................................................................................................................

...........................................................................................................................

...........................................................................................................................

...........................................................................................................................

...........................................................................................................................

...........................................................................................................................

...........................................................................................................................

...........................................................................................................................

...........................................................................................................................

...........................................................................................................................

...........................................................................................................................

# MEDICATIONS - ONE

Name: ......................................... Pharmacy: ...........................................

Drug Allergies: ...........................

| Drug Name | Treatment of | Started Taking | Dosage | How Often is the Drug Taken? | Prescribed by Whom? |
|---|---|---|---|---|---|
| | | | | | |
| | | | | | |
| | | | | | |
| | | | | | |
| | | | | | |
| | | | | | |
| | | | | | |
| | | | | | |
| | | | | | |
| | | | | | |
| | | | | | |
| | | | | | |

# MEDICATIONS - ONE

Name: .................................................. Pharmacy: ..................................................

Drug Allergies: ..................................................

| Drug Name | Treatment of | Started Taking | Dosage | How Often is the Drug Taken? | Prescribed by Whom? |
|-----------|--------------|----------------|--------|------------------------------|---------------------|
|           |              |                |        |                              |                     |
|           |              |                |        |                              |                     |
|           |              |                |        |                              |                     |
|           |              |                |        |                              |                     |
|           |              |                |        |                              |                     |
|           |              |                |        |                              |                     |
|           |              |                |        |                              |                     |
|           |              |                |        |                              |                     |
|           |              |                |        |                              |                     |
|           |              |                |        |                              |                     |
|           |              |                |        |                              |                     |
|           |              |                |        |                              |                     |
|           |              |                |        |                              |                     |

# MEDICAL INFORMATION - TWO

Name: .................................................................. Date ........................

Blood Type .................................. Height ........................ Weight ........................

**DOCTORS** *(General Practitioner, Dentist, Specialists, Audiology, Internist, Cardiology)*

Doctor: ............................................... Specialty: ..................................

Phone: .........................................................................

Doctor: ............................................... Specialty: ..................................

Phone: .........................................................................

Doctor: ............................................... Specialty: ..................................

Phone: .........................................................................

Doctor: ............................................... Specialty: ..................................

Phone: .........................................................................

* PATIENT PORTAL INFORMATION – add to PASSWORDS

Veterans Administration Facility: ................................ Phone: ..........................

.........................................................................................

Dentist: .............................................. Phone: ........................

Eye Doctor: ............................................. Phone: ........................

## MEDICAL EQUIPMENT

Do you use medical equipment? ................................ ..............................

Who is the supplier? ..........................................................................

Details? .........................................................................................

.........................................................................................

## MEDICAL CONDITIONS - TWO

Do you have any medical conditions or hereditary risk factors that require monitoring?

Please give details. ................................................................................
................................................................................
................................................................................
................................................................................
................................................................................

Do you have any allergies? Please give details.
................................................................................
................................................................................

## VACCINES AND IMMUNIZATIONS - Type and Date Received

................................................................................
................................................................................
................................................................................
................................................................................
................................................................................
................................................................................
................................................................................
................................................................................
................................................................................
................................................................................
................................................................................
................................................................................
................................................................................

# MEDICATIONS - TWO

Name: .....................  Pharmacy: .....................

Drug Allergies: .....................

| Drug Name | Treatment of | Started Taking | Dosage | How Often is the Drug Taken? | Prescribed by Whom? |
|-----------|--------------|----------------|--------|------------------------------|---------------------|
|           |              |                |        |                              |                     |
|           |              |                |        |                              |                     |
|           |              |                |        |                              |                     |
|           |              |                |        |                              |                     |
|           |              |                |        |                              |                     |
|           |              |                |        |                              |                     |
|           |              |                |        |                              |                     |
|           |              |                |        |                              |                     |
|           |              |                |        |                              |                     |
|           |              |                |        |                              |                     |
|           |              |                |        |                              |                     |
|           |              |                |        |                              |                     |

# MEDICATIONS - TWO

Name: ..............................................  Pharmacy: ..............................................

Drug Allergies: ..............................................

| Drug Name | Treatment of | Started Taking | Dosage | How Often is the Drug Taken? | Prescribed by Whom? |
|-----------|--------------|----------------|--------|------------------------------|---------------------|
|           |              |                |        |                              |                     |
|           |              |                |        |                              |                     |
|           |              |                |        |                              |                     |
|           |              |                |        |                              |                     |
|           |              |                |        |                              |                     |
|           |              |                |        |                              |                     |
|           |              |                |        |                              |                     |
|           |              |                |        |                              |                     |
|           |              |                |        |                              |                     |
|           |              |                |        |                              |                     |
|           |              |                |        |                              |                     |
|           |              |                |        |                              |                     |
|           |              |                |        |                              |                     |

# FINAL WISHES - ONE

## DESIGNATIONS

Do you want to designate someone to carry out your wishes for your funeral?  Y/N

If yes, who and have you discussed your wishes with them? .................................

Do you have money set aside for your funeral?  If yes, where? .............................

..................................................................................................

What is your choice for the final disposition of your body?

Burial-traditional in-ground: ...................      Burial-above ground: ......................

Burial-green:  ........................................      Cremation-traditional: .....................

Placement of cremation ashes? .......................................................................

..................................................................................................

## RELIGIOUS OR MEMORIAL SERVICE

Type of Service: ................................ ...................... Location ..........................

Officiant Name: ................................ Phone Number: .............................

## FUNERAL HOME

Funeral Home Preference: ...........................................................................

Contact Name: ..................................... Phone Number: .............................

Have you purchased a package from the funeral home?  Y/N

## CEMETERY

Cemetery Name: .....................................................................................

I have a plot in the name of: ......................... The deed is stored: .......................

I am entitled to military honors: Y/N      I am entitled to Veteran's benefits: Y/N

## NOTES: ..........................................................................................

..................................................................................................

..................................................................................................

## VIEWING

If there is a casket, would you like a viewing?

.................................................................................................

## OBITUARY

Would you like to write your Obituary, or is there something you want to be mentioned in your Obituary? If so, write it on a separate sheet and add it to the end of the book.

## SERVICE

Would you like a religious service or a memorial service?
.................................................................................................

Where would you like the service to be held?
.................................................................................................

Please describe the mood or tone of the service you'd like to have.
.................................................................................................

What hymns or music would you like to be played?
.................................................................................................

Which Bible verses, poetry, or readings would you like to have read?
.................................................................................................

Who would you like to speak?
.................................................................................................

Do you have photos or other remembrances that you'd like displayed? Please describe.
.................................................................................................

Would you like to specify a charity in place of flowers?
.................................................................................................

Would you like to give your guests something at the service, such as a program, memorial card, photograph, or bookmark?
.................................................................................................

Please identify specific people, if any, that you want to be sure are invited to your service.

.................................................................................................

.................................................................................................

.................................................................................................

.................................................................................................

.................................................................................................

## MILITARY HONORS

If you are entitled to military honors, a flag presentation, and playing "Taps," would you like to have the benefits? ........................................................................................................

## GRAVESIDE

Would you like everyone to be invited to the graveside? ........................................................

Have you purchased a headstone? ........................................................................................

What type of headstone would you like to have, and what would you like engraved on it? ....................................................................................................................................
........................................................................................................................................

Would you like to specify a special reading? ........................................................................

Is there someone you would like to speak? ........................................................................
........................................................................................................................................

Would you like people to place something on your casket? ..................................................

## RECEPTION

Where would you like the reception to be held? ..................................................................
........................................................................................................................................

Who would you like to be invited? ......................................................................................
........................................................................................................................................
........................................................................................................................................

## POST-RECEPTION ACTIVITY

Would you like your friends and loved ones to do something together or individually to honor you? Ideas: a memorial scholarship, taking a walk, stories, etc.
........................................................................................................................................
........................................................................................................................................

Additional wishes and thoughts:
........................................................................................................................................
........................................................................................................................................
........................................................................................................................................
........................................................................................................................................
........................................................................................................................................

# FINAL WISHES - TWO

## DESIGNATIONS

Do you want to designate someone to carry out your wishes for your funeral?  Y/N

If yes, who and have you discussed your wishes with them? ................................

Do you have money set aside for your funeral?  If yes, where? ...........................

...........................................................................................................................

What is your choice for the final disposition of your body?

Burial-traditional in-ground: ...................     Burial-above ground: ......................

Burial-green:  ........................................     Cremation-traditional: ....................

Placement of cremation ashes? ........................................................................

...........................................................................................................................

## RELIGIOUS OR MEMORIAL SERVICE

Type of Service: .................................. ...................... Location ...........................

Officiant Name: ......................................... Phone Number: .............................

## FUNERAL HOME

Funeral Home Preference: ...............................................................................

Contact Name: ........................................ Phone Number: ..............................

Have you purchased a package from the funeral home?  Y/N

## CEMETERY

Cemetery Name: ............................................................................................

I have a plot in the name of: .......................... The deed is stored: .......................

I am entitled to military honors: Y/N      I am entitled to Veteran's benefits: Y/N

## NOTES: ......................................................................................

...........................................................................................................................

...........................................................................................................................

## VIEWING

If there is a casket, would you like a viewing?

..........................................................................................................................

## OBITUARY

Would you like to write your Obituary, or is there something you want to be mentioned in your Obituary? If so, write it on a separate sheet and add it to the end of the book.

## SERVICE

Would you like a religious service or a memorial service?

..........................................................................................................................

Where would you like the service to be held?

..........................................................................................................................

Please describe the mood or tone of the service you'd like to have.

..........................................................................................................................

What hymns or music would you like to be played?

..........................................................................................................................

Which Bible verses, poetry, or readings would you like to have read?

..........................................................................................................................

Who would you like to speak?

..........................................................................................................................

Do you have photos or other remembrances that you'd like displayed? Please describe.

..........................................................................................................................

Would you like to specify a charity in place of flowers?

..........................................................................................................................

Would you like to give your guests something at the service, such as a program, memorial card, photograph, or bookmark?

..........................................................................................................................

Please identify specific people, if any, that you want to be sure are invited to your service.

..........................................................................................................................

..........................................................................................................................

..........................................................................................................................

..........................................................................................................................

..........................................................................................................................

## MILITARY HONORS

If you are entitled to military honors, a flag presentation, and playing "Taps," would you like to have the benefits? ..............................................................................

## GRAVESIDE

Would you like everyone to be invited to the graveside? ........................................

Have you purchased a headstone? ..........................................................................

What type of headstone would you like to have, and what would you like engraved on it? ....................................................................................................................
..............................................................................................................................

Would you like to specify a special reading? .......................................................

Is there someone you would like to speak? ..........................................................
..............................................................................................................................

Would you like people to place something on your casket? ...................................

## RECEPTION

Where would you like the reception to be held? ...................................................
..............................................................................................................................

Who would you like to be invited? ........................................................................
..............................................................................................................................
..............................................................................................................................

## POST-RECEPTION ACTIVITY

Would you like your friends and loved ones to do something together or individually to honor you? Ideas: a memorial scholarship, taking a walk, stories, etc.

..............................................................................................................................
..............................................................................................................................

Additional wishes and thoughts:

..............................................................................................................................
..............................................................................................................................
..............................................................................................................................
..............................................................................................................................
..............................................................................................................................

# PASSWORDS - ONE

Name: ..............

| Company / Site Address | User ID | Password |
|---|---|---|
| Cell Phone | | |
| Computer | | |
| | | |
| | | |
| | | |
| | | |
| | | |
| | | |
| | | |
| | | |
| | | |
| | | |
| | | |

# PASSWORDS - ONE

Name: .........................................

| Company / Site Address | User ID | Password |
|---|---|---|
| | | |
| | | |
| | | |
| | | |
| | | |
| | | |
| | | |
| | | |
| | | |
| | | |
| | | |
| | | |
| | | |
| | | |

# PASSWORDS - TWO

Name: ........................................................

| Company / Site Address | User ID | Password |
|---|---|---|
| Cell Phone | | |
| Computer | | |
| | | |
| | | |
| | | |
| | | |
| | | |
| | | |
| | | |
| | | |
| | | |
| | | |
| | | |

# PASSWORDS - TWO

Name: ................

| Company / Site Address | User ID | Password |
|---|---|---|
| | | |
| | | |
| | | |
| | | |
| | | |
| | | |
| | | |
| | | |
| | | |
| | | |
| | | |
| | | |
| | | |

# MONTHLY BILLS

Company: ............................................. Phone number: ...........................

Account number: ................................... Contact name: ............................

Bill received by mail or email: ..................................................................

What address: ............................................................................................

How do you pay? ............................................. *Check, Website, Auto-Debit

How often do you pay? ................................. What amount? ...................

*Full, Minimum, Other

---

Company: ............................................. Phone number: ...........................

Account number: ................................... Contact name: ............................

Bill received by mail or email: ..................................................................

What address: ............................................................................................

How do you pay? ............................................. *Check, Website, Auto-Debit

How often do you pay? ................................. What amount? ...................

*Full, Minimum, Other

---

Company: ............................................. Phone number: ...........................

Account number: ................................... Contact name: ............................

Bill received by mail or email: ..................................................................

What address: ............................................................................................

How do you pay? ............................................. *Check, Website, Auto-Debit

How often do you pay? ................................. What amount? ...................

*Full, Minimum, Other

---

Company: ............................................. Phone number: ...........................

Account number: ................................... Contact name: ............................

Bill received by mail or email: ..................................................................

What address: ............................................................................................

How do you pay? ............................................. *Check, Website, Auto-Debit

How often do you pay? ................................. What amount? ...................

# MONTHLY BILLS

Company: ..................................................... Phone number: ................................

Account number: ....................................... Contact name: ...............................

Bill received by mail or email: ..........................................................................

What address: .......................................................................................................

How do you pay? ......................................................... *Check, Website, Auto-Debit

How often do you pay? ................................................ What amount? ...................

*Full, Minimum, Other

---

Company: ..................................................... Phone number: ................................

Account number: ....................................... Contact name: ...............................

Bill received by mail or email: ..........................................................................

What address: .......................................................................................................

How do you pay? ......................................................... *Check, Website, Auto-Debit

How often do you pay? ................................................ What amount? ...................

*Full, Minimum, Other

---

Company: ..................................................... Phone number: ................................

Account number: ....................................... Contact name: ...............................

Bill received by mail or email: ..........................................................................

What address: .......................................................................................................

How do you pay? ......................................................... *Check, Website, Auto-Debit

How often do you pay? ................................................ What amount? ...................

*Full, Minimum, Other

---

Company: ..................................................... Phone number: ................................

Account number: ....................................... Contact name: ...............................

Bill received by mail or email: ..........................................................................

What address: .......................................................................................................

How do you pay? ......................................................... *Check, Website, Auto-Debit

How often do you pay? ................................................ What amount? ...................

# MONTHLY BILLS

Company: ..................................................... Phone number: ...............................

Account number: ........................................ Contact name: ...............................

Bill received by mail or email: .........................................................................

What address: ..................................................................................................

How do you pay? ....................................................... *Check, Website, Auto-Debit

How often do you pay? ................................................ What amount? ..................

*Full, Minimum, Other

---

Company: ..................................................... Phone number: ...............................

Account number: ........................................ Contact name: ...............................

Bill received by mail or email: .........................................................................

What address: ..................................................................................................

How do you pay? ....................................................... *Check, Website, Auto-Debit

How often do you pay? ................................................ What amount? ..................

*Full, Minimum, Other

---

Company: ..................................................... Phone number: ...............................

Account number: ........................................ Contact name: ...............................

Bill received by mail or email: .........................................................................

What address: ..................................................................................................

How do you pay? ....................................................... *Check, Website, Auto-Debit

How often do you pay? ................................................ What amount? ..................

*Full, Minimum, Other

---

If you have additional monthly bills, write them on a
separate sheet of paper and store them inside this book.

# SUBSCRIPTIONS, MEMBERSHIPS, AND PUBLICATIONS

*Make a list of all your online and print accounts with dues or payments. You may add log-in information here or on the password page.*

..................................................................................................................

..................................................................................................................

..................................................................................................................

..................................................................................................................

..................................................................................................................

..................................................................................................................

..................................................................................................................

..................................................................................................................

..................................................................................................................

..................................................................................................................

..................................................................................................................

..................................................................................................................

..................................................................................................................

..................................................................................................................

..................................................................................................................

..................................................................................................................

..................................................................................................................

..................................................................................................................

..................................................................................................................

..................................................................................................................

..................................................................................................................

..................................................................................................................

..................................................................................................................

..................................................................................................................

..................................................................................................................

..................................................................................................................

..................................................................................................................

..................................................................................................................

# IF I'M UNABLE TO COMMUNICATE, - ONE

*please take care of the following items:*

........................................................................................................................................

........................................................................................................................................

........................................................................................................................................

........................................................................................................................................

........................................................................................................................................

........................................................................................................................................

........................................................................................................................................

........................................................................................................................................

........................................................................................................................................

........................................................................................................................................

........................................................................................................................................

........................................................................................................................................

........................................................................................................................................

........................................................................................................................................

........................................................................................................................................

........................................................................................................................................

........................................................................................................................................

........................................................................................................................................

........................................................................................................................................

........................................................................................................................................

........................................................................................................................................

........................................................................................................................................

# ADDITIONAL INFORMATION - ONE

*Include anything that is not covered in any other section.*

# IF I'M UNABLE TO COMMUNICATE, - TWO

*please take care of the following items:*

..........................................................................................................................

..........................................................................................................................

..........................................................................................................................

..........................................................................................................................

..........................................................................................................................

..........................................................................................................................

..........................................................................................................................

..........................................................................................................................

..........................................................................................................................

..........................................................................................................................

..........................................................................................................................

..........................................................................................................................

..........................................................................................................................

..........................................................................................................................

..........................................................................................................................

..........................................................................................................................

..........................................................................................................................

..........................................................................................................................

..........................................................................................................................

..........................................................................................................................

..........................................................................................................................

..........................................................................................................................

# ADDITIONAL INFORMATION - TWO

*Include anything that is not covered in any other section.*

# ADDITIONAL INFORMATION

*Include anything that is not covered in any other section.*

# PET INFORMATION

Pet Name: ............................. Date of Birth: ...................... Age: .................

Breed: ...................................... Coat Color: ................................

☐ Canine/Dog ☐ Feline/Cat ☐ Neutered or Spayed Other: .......................

Notable markings on pet: ..............................................................

Veterinarian name and phone number: ...........................................

..........................................................................................

24-hour Veterinarian name and phone number: ...............................

..........................................................................................

Is this a service animal with certification? ....................................

Where do you keep the certification document? ..............................

Any Medical or Behavioral Alerts? Seizures, caution with humans or other animals, adverse reactions to medications, allergies, blind, or deaf. ...................................

..........................................................................................

..........................................................................................

## IDENTIFICATION

Does your pet have identification tags with your name and phone number? Y/N

What name and number are on the tags? ........................................

..........................................................................................

Does your pet have a microchip or tattoo? ....................................

..........................................................................................

What is the number? ....................................................................

..........................................................................................

Local shelter name and phone number: ..........................................

..........................................................................................

Local shelter name and phone number: ..........................................

..........................................................................................

## VACCINES

*Common Vaccines: Bordetella, Lepto, DHPP, DHLPP, Rattlesnake, FVRCP, Feline Leukemia*

Date of Last Rabies Vaccine: ..............................................................................

Name of Vaccine: ........................................... Date: ............................

Name of Vaccine: ........................................... Date: ............................

Name of Vaccine: ........................................... Date: ............................

Name of Vaccine: ........................................... Date: ............................

Name of Vaccine: ........................................... Date: ............................

Name of Vaccine: ........................................... Date: ............................

## MEDICATIONS

Is your pet on medications? ..........................................................................

Name of medications: ....................................................................................

....................................................................................................................

Where do you purchase the medications? ....................................................

....................................................................................................................

If online, what is the website and account information?................................

....................................................................................................................

Account User ID: ..................................... Password: ............................

Are your orders on auto-delivery? ................................................................

....................................................................................................................

Additional notes: ...........................................................................................

....................................................................................................................

## INSURANCE

Do you have pet insurance? ..............................................................................

..........................................................................................................................

What is the company name and policy number? ...................................................

..........................................................................................................................

..........................................................................................................................

## PET CARE SERVICE

List the name of the people or companies you use for pet care: walking, feeding, or overnights.

Name: ........................................................ Phone Number: ............................

Name: ........................................................ Phone Number: ............................

## LONG-TERM CARE PLANNING

Have you designated someone to care for your pet if you are unable? ......................

Name and contact information: ..........................................................................

..........................................................................................................................

Details of the arrangement: ..............................................................................

..........................................................................................................................

..........................................................................................................................

..........................................................................................................................

Have you done estate planning for your pet and included it as part of your Will? .........

Details of the arrangement: ..............................................................................

..........................................................................................................................

..........................................................................................................................

..........................................................................................................................

Additional notes about your pet: ........................................................................

..........................................................................................................................

# LETTER TO A LOVED ONE

# LETTER TO A LOVED ONE

# LETTER TO A LOVED ONE

# LETTER TO A LOVED ONE

........................................................................................................

........................................................................................................

........................................................................................................

........................................................................................................

........................................................................................................

........................................................................................................

........................................................................................................

........................................................................................................

........................................................................................................

........................................................................................................

........................................................................................................

........................................................................................................

........................................................................................................

........................................................................................................

........................................................................................................

........................................................................................................

........................................................................................................

........................................................................................................

........................................................................................................

........................................................................................................

........................................................................................................

........................................................................................................

........................................................................................................

........................................................................................................

........................................................................................................

Made in the USA
Middletown, DE
20 December 2023

46375845R00046